D1567278

SAGEBRUSH AND PAINTBRUSH

THE STORY OF CHARLIE RUSSELL, THE COWBOY ARTIST

BY NANCY PLAIN

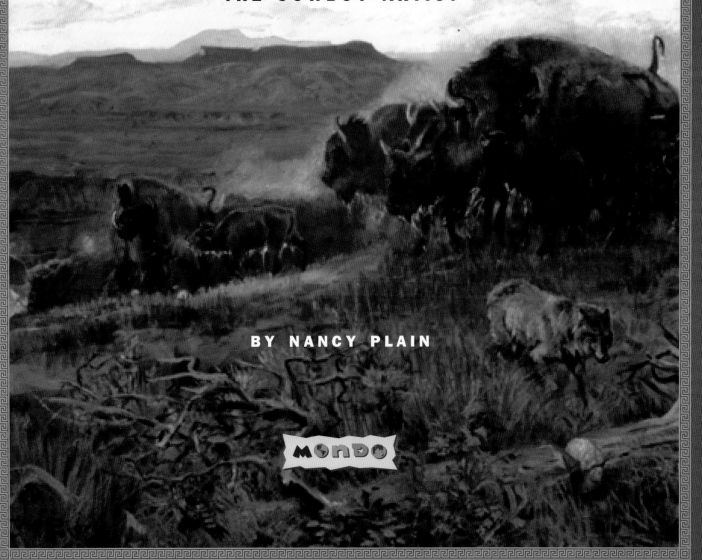

MONDO

For Sarah, Katherine, Andrew, and Amy—N.P.

TEXT COPYRIGHT © 2007 by Nancy Plain

PHOTOGRAPHY AND ARTWORK CREDITS
Every effort has been made to trace the ownership of all copyright materials in this book and to obtain permission for their use.

Front cover (t), p. 7: *Salute to the Robe Trade*, Gilcrease Museum, Tulsa, Oklahoma; front cover (b), pp. 11, 13, 16, 29: Courtesy Sid Richardson Collection of Western Art, Fort Worth, Texas; pp. 2, 7 (background), 13 (background), 25, 39: Charles M. Russell, *Before the White Man Came*, ca. 1922, Pen & ink graphite on paper, 1961.318, Amon Carter Museum, Fort Worth, Texas; p. 5: Charles M. Russell, *Charlie Himself*, ca. 1915, Wax, cloth, plaster, metal, string, and paint, 1961.58, Amon Carter Museum, Fort Worth, Texas; pp. 10, 17: Courtesy Buffalo Bill Historical Center; p. 16 Charles M. Russell, *Indian on Horseback*, 1907, Transparent and opaque watercolor over graphite underdrawing on paperboard, 1961.156, Amon Carter Museum, Fort Worth, Texas; p. 19: Charles M. Russell, *Breaking Camp*, ca.1885, Oil on canvas, 1961.145, Amon Carter Museum, Fort Worth, Texas; p. 21: Charles M. Russell, *Cowboy Camp During the Roundup*, ca.1885-1887, Oil on canvas, 1961.186, Amon Carter Museum, Fort Worth, Texas; pp. 1, 22, 23, 36, 41, 44-45: Courtesy Montana Historical Society; p. 26: Charles M. Russell, *Bronc in Cow Camp*, 1897, Oil on canvas, 1961.144, Amon Carter Museum, Fort Worth, Texas; p. 27: Charles M. Russell, *The Hold Up*, 1899, Oil on canvas, 1961.212, Amon Carter Museum, Fort Worth, Texas; p. 28: Charles Marion Russell, *Buffalo Hunt*, 1897, Oil on canvas, Private Collection, Bridgeman Art Library; p. 31: Charles M. Russell, *Smoking Up*, 1904, Bronze, 1961.83, Amon Carter Museum, Fort Worth, Texas; p. 32: Charles M. Russell, *Sleeping Thunder*, 1901, Bronze, 1961.105, Amon Carter Museum, Fort Worth, Texas; p. 33: Charles M. Russell, *Sun Worship in Montana*, 1907, Opaque and transparent watercolor over graphite underdrawing on paper, 1961.150, Amon Carter Museum, Fort Worth, Texas; pp. 34, 46-47: Charles M. Russell, *The Medicine Man*, 1908, Oil on canvas, 1961.171, Amon Carter Museum, Fort Worth, Texas; p. 40: Courtesy of the Eiteljorg Museum of American Indians and Western Art; p. 42: Charles M. Russell, *Smoke of a .45*, 1908, Oil on canvas, 1961.205, Amon Carter Museum, Fort Worth, Texas.

ALL RIGHTS RESERVED. No part of this publication may be reproduced, except in the case of quotation for articles or reviews, or stored in any retrieval system, or transmitted in any form or by any means, electronic, mechanical, photocopying, recording, or otherwise, without written permission from the publisher.

FOR INFORMATION CONTACT:
MONDO Publishing
980 Avenue of the Americas
New York, NY 10018
Visit our website at www.mondopub.com

Printed in China
09 10 11 12 13   9 8 7 6 5 4 3 2
ISBN 1-59336-729-5 (PB)

COVER AND BOOK DESIGN BY Michelle Farinella

Library of Congress Cataloging-in-Publication Data available upon request

CONTENTS

———— ◦●◦ ————

A Nighthawk

It was night, and the big sky over Montana Territory glittered with the cold light of a million stars. A young cowboy named Charlie Russell was on "nighthawk" duty for a cattle roundup. On his spotted pony, Monte, he watched over the horse herd, circling and circling as the animals grazed and slept. To keep them calm, he sang a cowboy tune. Charlie didn't mind riding all night. He would catch up on sleep in the morning, when the other men were out on the range chasing cattle. Besides, the sunrise over the mountains, the way light and color moved across the prairie, was a treat to see.

Charlie was new to the roundup, but already he felt at home. This wasn't because he was a first-rate roper or rider. He wasn't. In fact, he was afraid of bucking broncos. But he liked life on the range, and he made friends easily. Around the campfire he told stories that made the other cowboys roar with laughter. And always, as he talked, he would pull a lump of beeswax from his pocket and make little figures—Indians, cowboys, outlaws, animals—whatever characters he needed to illustrate his tales.

It seemed that Charlie could draw or paint anything, too. Wherever he

went, his pencils and paints went with him, stuffed into a spare sock.

The cowboys recognized their faces in his

pictures, which he dashed off on scraps of

paper, bits of wood, even the lining of

someone's hat. In a few years, this habit of

sketching life on the range would earn

Charlie the nickname the Cowboy Artist,

and he would become famous throughout

the country. But in 1882, his first year as a

wrangler, he was just that newcomer,

"Kid" Russell. He was a long way from his hometown of

St. Louis, Missouri, but Montana was where he wanted to be. ✷

"Charlie Himself"

Charlie was a dreamer. On horseback he pretended to be a cowboy or an Indian, riding out on the western frontier—the windblown prairie or the steep trails of the mountains.

CHAPTER ONE

DAYDREAMER

Charles Marion Russell was born in St. Louis, Missouri, on March 19, 1864, one year before the end of the Civil War. In a family that would grow to include six children, Charlie was third in line. When he was five years old, his parents, Charles Silas and Mary, moved their brood to Oak Hill, the Russell family property outside of St. Louis. There Charlie, his sister, and four brothers would grow up, surrounded by aunts, uncles, and cousins of all ages.

Oak Hill was rich in coal and underground deposits of clay, and the family mining business flourished. While the coal supplied St. Louis with fuel, the clay, used to make bricks and tile, helped build the growing city. The Parker-Russell Mining and Manufacturing Company was one of the largest of its kind in America.

Oak Hill was beautiful, too, with woods and fields, apple orchards and meadows, even vineyards that the Russells tended so they could make their own wine. When Charlie was eight, he was given a pony named Gyp. Soon he was riding bareback, exploring the land at a gallop—as his sister, Susan, wrote, "going like the wind."

Charlie was a dreamer. On horseback he pretended to be a cowboy or an Indian, riding out on the western frontier—the windblown prairie or the steep trails of the mountains. His imagination grew rich with the stories that his father read aloud about the lives of the pioneer Daniel Boone, the woodsman Davy Crockett, the wilderness scout Kit Carson. When he was old enough, Charlie began to read books on his own and never stopped. One that he especially enjoyed was the life story of William F. Cody, better known as "Buffalo Bill," the buffalo hunter and showman who toured the world with his famous Wild West Show.

Among Charlie's favorite stories were the ones about his own relatives. His great-uncle George Bent was one of the early fur traders in the Montana region. His great-uncles William and Charles Bent were traders and explorers who were even more important figures in the history of the American West. In the 1820s they helped establish the Santa Fe Trail, which began in Missouri

Salute to the Robe Trade

and ended in what is now the state of New Mexico. The trail opened huge areas of the southwest to miners, settlers, and more traders and explorers. On the trail, in what is now Colorado, Charlie's great-uncles built a trading post called Bent's Fort. Every year more and more wagon trains loaded with trade goods rattled along the route to the fort, until it became the main place to do business in the region.

William Bent married a Cheyenne Indian named Owl Woman. Two of the couple's sons, George and Charles, chose to live with their mother's people as members of the southern Cheyenne group. These men were Charlie's distant cousins. The more he learned about Western history and his own family ties, the more he wanted to see the West for himself. Secretly he started saving his allowance to pay for the trip he was sure he would make one day.

Charlie's daydreams soon found their way onto paper. "It was just kind of natural for me to draw pictures, I guess," he would recall one day. "I don't remember when I wasn't scratching around with a pencil." His favorite subject was horses. He drew them racing into battle with Indian warriors on their backs. He drew them carrying cowboys to the corral. And he drew them simply standing alone.

When he was very young, too, Charlie began sculpting with beeswax (modeling clay had not yet been invented). To the amusement of his family, he modeled all kinds of people and animals. Charlie's pocket-size horses had tails made from paintbrush bristles and little sticks for legs. With practice he would learn to model so well that he could do it without even looking. Charlie made larger sculptures, too, and won prizes for them at a St. Louis art fair two years in a row.

Horses and adventure stories and artwork made Charlie happy. School did not. His teachers thought he was "hopeless" because he never learned the rules of spelling or punctuation. His handwriting was a mess. Instead of trying harder, Charlie spent his time making beeswax animals and doodling in his school books. He swapped his sketches for other students' homework. "You get my lesson for me and I'll make you two Indians," he would say to his friends. Funny pictures that he drew of his teachers just made them more upset with him. Charlie played hooky all the time.

Many of his "vacation days" were spent at the St. Louis riverfront, on the banks of the Mississippi River. This was the place from which the Lewis and Clark Expedition had set out in 1804, and it was still the place where most trips west began. From St. Louis, steamboats headed up the Mississippi to the Missouri River. The wide Missouri—the "Big Muddy"—was the travelers' path to the Great Plains, that region of grassland that sweeps westward from the river all the way to the Rocky Mountains.

For centuries the Great Plains had been home to Native Americans and to the immense herds of buffalo that they followed for food. (Although *bison* is the correct scientific name, the word *buffalo* was commonly used by settlers to refer to the large, shaggy-headed animals that once roamed the North American prairie. *Buffalo* is, therefore, used at times in this book.) In the early 1800s, though, small groups of white explorers, fur trappers, and traders began to try their luck in the western wilderness. By the end of the Civil War in 1865, when Charlie was just a baby, many thousands of people were moving west. They came from the eastern United States, and they also came from Europe. They came to mine for gold, they came to farm or raise cattle and sheep, and they came to build the railroads. As the railroads made their way little by little across the prairie, towns sprang up alongside the tracks.

Unfortunately the newcomers were disturbing Indian lands and killing the sacred buffalo. All the Indian nations, from the Apaches on the southern plains to the Sioux in the north, fought to save their way of life. So began the Indian Wars, hundreds of battles between the Native Americans and the United States Army.

As young Charlie wandered the riverfront, he saw the people who were journeying back and forth from the frontier. He heard them talk of Indians and of the wild land that was so vast that it seemed endless. Since the Homestead Act of 1862, when the government had offered free land to anyone willing to farm it, "Western fever" had only increased. Charlie had a bad case of it.

His parents still hoped that he would finish school and perhaps join the family business. They enrolled him in art school in St. Louis. After a couple of

The
Buffalo Herd

days, he quit. When he was fifteen, they sent him to military school. He quit that, too. The Russells finally gave up. They arranged for Charlie to go west with a man named Pike Miller, who owned a sheep ranch in Montana Territory. The hard work of a ranch hand would send their son rushing back to comfortable St. Louis, the Russells thought. But for Charlie, this was the adventure he'd been waiting for, the only thing he wanted for his sixteenth birthday. ✷

The Scout

Dressed in a buckskin shirt and cowboy boots,
he looked to his family like a real Westerner.
He talked like one now, too.

CHAPTER TWO

"KID" RUSSELL

In March 1880 Charlie and Pike traveled by train and bumpy stagecoach to the town of Helena, in Montana Territory. (In 1880 only about half
of the country west of the Mississippi River was organized into states; the other
half was divided into territories.) Helena had begun as a gold-mining camp
during the Montana gold rush of the 1860s. Last Chance Gulch it was called
then. By the time Charlie arrived, Helena was the capital of the Territory. Pike's
sheep ranch was still far away—a long ride over the prairie to a part of central
Montana called the Judith Basin.

The Judith Basin was so called after the river that flows through it—the
Judith, named by William Clark as the Lewis and Clark Expedition passed
through Montana in 1805. The Basin is a wide stretch of rolling prairie
surrounded by mountains—the Highwoods, the Judiths, the Big Snowies, and
the Little Belts. When Charlie first saw the Basin, few people lived there. Mostly
it was home to antelope, elk, deer, coyotes, wolves, and bears. There were
forests of pine and aspen trees. Cottonwood trees grew near sparkling streams.
In spring and summer, wildflowers bloomed amid sagebrush and grasses.

The Judith country had until recently been the land of the Piegan Indians, one of the three branches of the once-powerful Blackfeet nation. But in the 1870s the United States Army had finally won the Indian Wars. All the native peoples of the West, including those in Montana, had been forced onto parcels of land called reservations. In those areas, they were poor and sometimes starving, so they often left to wander their old hunting grounds in search of food or horses. On his way to Pike's ranch, Charlie met one such group of Crow Indians riding by.

The Basin, like the rest of the West, had also recently belonged to the buffalo. There had been many millions of them grazing peacefully on the plains. The Native Americans believed the big, shaggy-headed animals were a gift from the Great Spirit. They provided the people with meat, hides, and almost everything else they needed to live. But as white settlers moved west, they

The Snow Trail

began to kill the buffalo. Then in the 1870s and early 1880s, the trains brought hunters with powerful rifles, who slaughtered almost every last one. When Charlie first came to the Judith country, he might have seen a few buffalo, but by the mid-1880s, there would be only a few hundred left in all the West. Their bones lay in piles on the prairie.

At Pike's ranch, Charlie discovered that he did not "get along at all well" with the sheep. He kept losing track of them because he was so busy sketching the scenery. At the same time, Pike discovered that he did not get along with his new sheepherder. Charlie was lazy, Pike thought, and "ornery"—not even "worth his grub." Charlie was quickly fired. He saddled his brown mare and packed his bedroll on Monte, the new pony that he had bought from some Piegan Indians. Then he rode off to find another job.

At nightfall, jobless and very hungry, he camped by the Judith River. "A man never needed a friend worse than I did," he later remembered. "I felt mighty blue." Then along came someone named Jake Hoover, riding a horse called Guts. Jake was one of the last of the oldtime mountain men. He was a hunter and trapper who sold meat, furs, and hides to the few ranchers and miners in the region. His home base was a cabin in a part of the Judith country called Pig Eye Basin. If Charlie would help with his hunting operation, Jake said, he could have plenty of food and a place to live. That settled it for Charlie.

Pig Eye Basin was an unforgettable place. When Charlie saw it, he thought that "no king of the old times could have claimed a more beautiful and bountiful domain." Located on a fork of the Judith River, Jake's cabin had a dirt floor and homemade furniture. It sat amid meadows, forested foothills, and creeks full of trout. Wild animals were all around. From Jake, Charlie learned how to take care of himself in the wilderness. From the animals, he learned to be a better artist, drawing them and modeling them in clay every chance he could get. The magnificent Pig Eye was better than college or art school for Charlie. He spent much of the next two years helping Jake around the cabin, going with him on hunting trips, and listening to the mountain man's many stories. And he remembered every one.

In 1882 Charlie returned to St. Louis for the first time since he had gone west. Dressed in a buckskin shirt and cowboy boots, he looked to his family like a real Westerner. He talked like one now, too. If the Russells suspected that they had lost him to Montana, they were right. Charlie would never live in St. Louis again, but only go back from time to time to visit. After a month in the city, he loaded up on art supplies and headed back to his adopted home.

On the way back to Jake's cabin, Charlie met a bunch of cowboys who were driving 1,000 head of cattle to the roundup in the Judith Basin. The boss of this cow company, or outfit, hired Charlie to herd the men's horses at night during the trail drive. This was his first cowboy job. It was more fun than herd-ing sheep, and he performed his nighthawk duties well.

The Deer in the Forest

Indian on Horseback

Charlie had come to Montana just as the cattle industry was starting to take hold. In 1880 there were few herds in the Territory. But with the Native Americans on reservations and the bison gone, the prairie was wide open to cattlemen. They could fatten their animals for free. Soon hundreds of thousands of cattle came to graze on the rich Montana grass. Many of them were driven up on trails from the southern plains. "All the cattle in the world seemed to be coming up from Texas," noted one cowboy. The herds could wander for miles in any direction; there wasn't a fence in sight. Yet there was a limit to this seemingly endless space. By the mid-1880s, the range would become overcrowded.

There were two roundup times each year. In spring, cowboys separated, or cut out, the cattle of the various owners. When this was done, the men marked the new calves born on the open range with the brands of their owners. The herds were then set free again to graze. At the autumn roundup, cowboys gathered the cows that were to be sold for beef and drove them to the railroads for shipping to slaughter-

houses in Chicago and other cities. Cattlemen from all the outfits in a region *"Kid Russell" Photo* worked together each roundup season, forming associations such as the Bear Paw, the Moccasin, and the Judith roundups.

Soon after Charlie's first trail drive, the boss of the Judith Roundup, Horace Brewster, hired him for his second nightherding job. This is how "Kid" Russell, the boy from St. Louis, became an honest-to-goodness cowboy, working the roundup every spring and fall. ✳

Everything that happened on the range was a subject for Charlie's art. He wasn't an expert painter yet, but his pictures were bursting with action, and they were set against a dramatic backdrop of prairie, mountains, and sky.

CHAPTER THREE

THE COWBOY ARTIST

In the spring, Charlie herded horses, and on the fall roundups, cattle. As a night wrangler, he usually worked with a partner. Charlie spent most of his time in the saddle, and there was nothing in the world he loved more than that. The cattle kings, or owners of the big outfits, were in the business to get rich. But cowboys like Charlie just wanted the freedom of life on the open range. They were willing to fight the rustlers, who stole cattle. They were willing to put up with heat and cold, storms and dust—as well as nervous cows that would stampede, as one cowboy wrote, "if you'd so much as blow your nose."

Charlie slept on the ground, rolled up in blankets. His meals were simple—beef, beans, bacon, and coffee. In his "warbag," or sack, he carried his belongings, including the sock that held his art supplies. In the winter, when cowboys were not needed on the range, Charlie and his friends lived together in various Montana towns such as Helena, Great Falls, and Cascade. Or they wandered from one ranch to another, where they were sure to get a free meal. "Riding the grub-line" they called it. They were almost always broke.

Horace Brewster said that Charlie was "the most popular kid on the range," and that "he never swung a mean loop in his life, never done dirt to man or animal. . . . " A cowboy named C. J. Ellis wrote about Charlie, "if he ever had an enemy I never met him." Charlie made lifelong friends on the Judith Roundup, and he knew how to keep them laughing. He played practical jokes, such as arranging buffalo horns on the head of a drunken cowboy, and other pranks to liven up the day. And no one could tell a story better than he. Charlie repeated tales he'd heard from the colorful Montana characters he had met—mountain men, Indians, stage drivers, preachers, and saloon keepers, to name a few. He entertained his friends with events from his own life, too. There was the time Jake Hoover's pet pig wrecked Jake's cabin and the time when Charlie, scared out of his wits, had to cook breakfast for an Indian who was passing through the Pig Eye. "He always saw the funny side of anything that happened, and if there was no funny side he made one," wrote Ellis.

Breaking Camp

Everything that happened on the range was a subject for Charlie's art. He wasn't an expert painter yet, but his pictures were bursting with action, and they were set against a dramatic backdrop of prairie, mountains, and sky.

Some of the earliest scenes are watercolors of cowboys swinging lassos as they gallop after runaway steers or horses. In 1885 Charlie began to experiment with oil paint. *Breaking Camp*, one of his first oils, shows a busy morning at the cow camp. The breakfast fire is still smoking, and some men are saddling up for the day's work, while others are already struggling to stay on their half-tamed broncos. When they saw the painting, the other wranglers were able to recognize each man and horse in the picture. Charlie was so pleased with *Breaking Camp* that he sent it to St. Louis to be shown at an art fair.

Another oil, *Cowboy Camp During the Roundup*, is a different, larger view of the Judith Roundup. The little cow town of Utica is in the background. As in most of Charlie's paintings, even the smallest details in this oil are true to life, from the cowboys' clothes to the brands on their animals.

Charlie worked at night, slept in the morning, and had the afternoon free for his art. He would sit on his bedroll or in the shade of a wagon to paint. The closest thing he had to a studio was his friend Jim Shelton's saloon, in Utica. There, using house paint, Charlie created a large western scene to hang over the bar. The young cowboy gladly gave away most of his pictures to his friends. Once in a while, he would sell one for ten dollars or so. But he would never sell to anyone he didn't like.

Everyone who saw his work could tell that Charlie was really living the life he painted. Each picture told a story of Montana. And on each picture, as on almost all those he would ever paint, he sketched what he called his trademark. It was a buffalo skull, a symbol of the passing of the old days, when the West was truly wild.

In the fall of 1886, a cowboy friend of Charlie's named Teddy Blue Abbott saw a white Arctic owl on the range. According to Native American

tradition, this is a sign that a very cold winter is on the way. In November it started to snow—and it kept on snowing. At Christmas a blizzard struck that lasted for days and drove temperatures as low as 60 degrees below zero. The wind blew snow and ice so furiously that it was hard to breathe and impossible to see. In January a warm wind called a chinook came swooping over the plains and melted the top layers of snow. But then the snowmelt froze into a solid sheet of ice with the storms of February. It was the worst winter that anyone in the West had ever seen. Teddy Blue called it "Hell without the heat."

Others called it the Big Die-Up. During a normal winter, cattle roaming the range could find enough grass to survive. But during this terrible season, animals could find neither food nor shelter. Desperate cows wandered into towns or staggered over the prairie for miles until they collapsed. When spring finally came, ranchers figured that at least 60 percent of Montana's cattle had starved or frozen to death. The bodies were everywhere. It was a tragedy that left people speechless.

Cowboy Camp During the Roundup

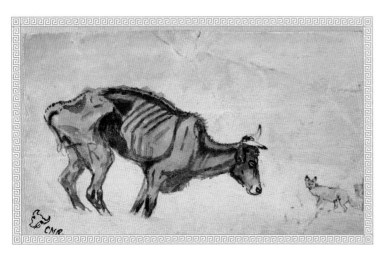

Waiting for a Chinook

Charlie spent that winter at a ranch owned by a man named Jesse Phelps. Jesse was in charge of a large herd whose owners lived in Helena. One day, Jesse wrote a letter to the owners to tell them how many cattle they had lost. To illustrate the note, Charlie took a piece of cardboard and made a quick watercolor sketch of a dying steer, its tail chewed by hungry wolves. *Waiting for a Chinook* he titled it. The little picture is only three inches high, but it powerfully sums up the horror of the Big Die-Up. The sketch attracted a lot of attention in Helena, and pretty soon, articles about Charlie were appearing in Montana newspapers. People began to call him the Cowboy Artist.

However, cowboy and cattle scenes were not all that Charlie painted. He was deeply interested in American Indians and their way of life. Was it because of his Cheyenne cousins in the Bent family? Or because he admired the freedom that the Plains Indians had once had? Charlie was keenly aware that the country had belonged first to the Indians, and he called them "the onley [sic] real Americans."

In 1888 a painting of Charlie's was reproduced for the first time in a national magazine, the popular *Harper's Weekly*. *Caught in the Act* shows a group of hungry Crow Indians who, having stolen and killed a cow, have been caught by two cowboys. Such situations were the bitter reality of Indian life in Charlie's day. Only a few years before he painted *Caught in the Act*, hundreds of Blackfeet men, women, and children had starved to death on a Montana reservation.

Charlie wanted to learn as much as possible about traditional tribal ways

before they disap-
peared altogether.
With two friends he
traveled to Alberta,
Canada, to spend the
summer of 1888 near
several reservations.
He visited Indian
lodges, attended
ceremonies, listened
to legends, and
practiced the sign
language that the
Plains people used
to communicate with

*Caught in
the Act*

each other. He made friends with a Blackfoot man named Absinkas and
sketched his portrait. In the fall Charlie returned to Montana with knowledge
that would enrich his art for the rest of his life.

Montana had changed since Charlie's first year in the Territory. Railroads
now crisscrossed the prairie. The population was booming. The Big Die-Up had
taught cattlemen to keep smaller herds and to fence them in so that they could
be fed during harsh winters. The Judith Basin itself was filling up with ranches,
farms, and even towns. "Nesters" Charlie called the settlers, and he was sad to
see farmers plowing up the prairie grass to plant their crops.

Because of the shrinking of open range land, in 1889 Charlie and the
other cowboys of the Judith Roundup were forced to drive their herds farther
north, to graze near the Canadian border. This was the last big area of unfenced
grassland in the Territory. That same year Montana became a state, the forty-
first in the union. ✳

Charlie rode the roundup and painted whenever and wherever he could. Oils and watercolors by the Cowboy Artist were now hanging on walls all over Montana—in hotels and ranch houses, stores and saloons.

CHAPTER FOUR

"WE ARE PARTNERS"

As the days of the sparsely populated open range game to an end, Charlie thought seriously about becoming a fulltime artist. But he did not think he could "make it stick," he told a friend. "I expect I will have to ride till the end of my days, but I would rather be a poor cow puncher than a poor artist." For a while he was both.

Charlie rode the roundup and painted whenever and wherever he could. Oils and watercolors by the Cowboy Artist were now hanging on walls all over Montana—in hotels and ranch houses, stores and saloons. Charlie even painted a cowboy scene on the door of a bank vault, for a $25 fee. He was, in the words of one friend, a "sagebrush celebrity."

But he was still broke, still selling pictures for a few dollars each or trading them to pay his bills. One blustery winter he shared a cabin with a group of friends who called themselves the Hungry Seven. Anytime Charlie sold a painting, he treated the Seven to dinner.

After the fall roundup of 1893, he rode with the beef cattle on the train to Chicago. There he bought himself a ticket to the most talked-about event of the year, the enormous Chicago World's Fair. Every state in the union had its own building at the fair, and Montana's displayed three paintings by Charlie. Mainly the fair was a celebration of American progress. New products—the first hamburger, the first dishwasher—made crowds of fairgoers excited about the future.

Not Charlie. He loved the old days and the old ways. Yet he could see that they would never come back. After his visit to Chicago, he quit the range forever. He had only been a cowboy for eleven years, or as he put it, "for 11 years I sung to their horses and cattle." But from then on, he would try to make a living by telling the story of the West through his art.

In 1895 in the little town of Cascade, Montana, Charlie was introduced to 17-year-old Nancy Cooper, nicknamed Mame. Although there was a big difference in their ages (Charlie was 31), someone who witnessed their meeting described it as "love at first sight." Years later, Nancy recalled her first impressions: Charlie in his Stetson hat, a red sash around his waist, rings on his fingers, and a twinkle in his gray-blue eyes. The couple were married in 1896. Their first home was a one-room cabin in their friends' backyard in Cascade. A year later, the newlyweds moved to the town of Great Falls, named for the waterfalls that had so amazed the men of the Lewis and Clark Expedition as they traveled the Missouri River.

"Life has never been too serious with me," Charlie once wrote. Luckily for him Nancy was as practical as he was playful. And she was determined. She encouraged him to work hard at his painting and stick to a schedule. She was good at finding buyers for his art, and she was never afraid to raise prices. In 1897 Charlie was shocked to receive $75 for an oil painting. "We are partners," he would gratefully say of Nancy one day. "She is the business end and I am the creative. . . ."

In his heart, however, Charlie was still a cowboy. His nearly perfect memory of his range days enabled him to create scene after scene. He painted cowboys roping and branding steers, chasing rustlers, and going a little wild on their free days in town. He especially enjoyed painting bucking broncos, and he often depicted horses and riders that he knew well. In *Bronc in Cow Camp*, Charlie's friend Bob tears through the campfire on a runaway horse named The Pinto. Breakfast is ruined!

Bronc in Cow Camp

Western history interested Charlie, too. He read and reread the journals that Lewis and Clark had written on their fantastic journey west. He painted a scene from the expedition—but from the Indians' point of view.

"No man ever lived long enough. . . to paint all the pictures I have in mind," Charlie told Nancy. He never ran out of ideas because he was a good listener. And in that time before television and movies, almost everyone had his or her own story to tell. Charlie based several paintings of outlaws on a real one named Big Nose George, who had robbed the Deadwood stagecoach in 1880. *The Hold Up* shows Big Nose's startled victims standing at gunpoint, their hands in the air. Charlie had heard about this robbery straight from some of the passengers themselves.

The Hold Up

But the Cowboy Artist's favorite subjects of all were Indians. During his career he would paint more Native American scenes than any other kind, and they would be among his most beautiful works. Charlie thought a lot about what had happened to the western Indian peoples. He had friends among the Blackfeet and the Cree. He had read and heard stories about the Indian Wars. "The history of how they fought for their country is written in blood, a stain that time cannot grinde [sic] out," Charlie strongly believed. It was an unusual opinion at a time when most white people in the West just wanted Indians to keep out of sight.

Charlie painted a portrait of almost every Native American in Montana that he knew. He visited different tribes and attended powwows to observe and to learn. As the years passed, he came to prefer showing the Indians as they had been when they ruled the Great Plains. He used his knowledge and

Buffalo
Hunt

imagination to paint scenes of Indian men in action—fighting, hunting, and riding, almost like knights in armor, over the land. Charlie had come West too late to see a buffalo hunt, but his pictures of them seem so real. One can almost hear the approaching thunder of the stampeding herds, the galloping horses. No wonder Charlie was called by one writer "one of the best animal painters in the world."

He was also one of the few Western artists who were fascinated by the lives of Indian women. He painted them at home preparing animal hides, braiding their husbands' hair, teaching their children. And he painted them performing one of their most important tasks—moving their villages from place to place. In *Bringing Up the Trail*, a woman on a white horse leads her people to a new campsite as a radiant sunset spreads its colors across the sky.

Charlie's art had come a long way since the rough sketches of his nighthawking days. With Nancy in charge of his career, he was painting more than ever before. He was also illustrating stories and articles for popular magazines. In 1900 the Russells moved to a bigger house in Great Falls, with a corral and a stable in the backyard. Three years later, Nancy had a studio built in the yard for Charlie—the first and only proper studio he had in his lifetime. It was made of telephone poles, log-cabin style. Charlie lovingly called it "the shack," and he filled it with all his Western treasures, from Indian pipes and moccasins to cowboys' spurs and saddles. These items came in handy as props for hundreds of paintings.

Charlie sketched and painted from early morning until noon. He hardly ever asked people to pose for him, sketching from memory instead. Sometimes he needed to be alone when painting, in a mood that Nancy called the "Great Silence." At other times he swapped stories with visitors as he sat at his easel. In the shack, Charlie felt closer to his cowboy days. He could even fry "campfire" meals and boil coffee for his guests in the room's big fireplace. "Come and get it," he would yell when dinner was ready.

Bringing Up the Trail

"I count all who love the old west [as] friends," he once wrote in a letter. Every afternoon he rode his horse downtown to the Mint or the Silver Dollar saloon to visit with "the bunch," his buddies from the range years. No matter how famous he became—and by 1900 his fame was spreading from the West to the rest of the country—Charlie never forgot an old friend. One of the oldest and best was his horse Monte, who had been with him since his first year in Montana. "We were kids together," Charlie wrote about his faithful pinto. "We have always been together. People who know me know him. We don't exactly talk to each other, but we sure savy [understand] one another." ✳

Until that time, everything Charlie knew about painting and drawing he had taught himself. What he learned from his friends in the New York art world allowed him—with plenty of hard work—to take a giant step forward.

THE "BIG CAMP"

Charlie did not like progress. He didn't like the electric lights, telephones, and automobiles of the new century. He called cars "skunk wagons" and refused to learn to drive. He wanted wilderness, not civilization. But since there were not enough art buyers in Montana to support his career, he had to visit the most crowded and civilized places of all—America's big, modern cities.

In 1903 after a stop in St. Louis, he and Nancy traveled to New York City. This was the first of many trips that they would take to this important center for art. To Charlie, New York was the "big camp," and its buildings were "tall tepees." In the city he was invited to share the studio of three well-known artists who admired his talent and enjoyed his stories.

Until that time, everything Charlie knew about painting and drawing he had taught himself. What he learned from his friends in the New York art world allowed him—with plenty of hard work—to take a giant step forward. He had already left behind the dark colors of his earliest paintings. But in New York he started to experiment even more with brighter, lighter colors, using glowing pinks, greens, and golden brown. The action in his pictures, always spirited, began to flow more smoothly. His drawing skills improved. And he became an expert at depicting mood, from extreme excitement to stillness and peace. The more Charlie learned, the higher he set his standards.

While Charlie traded tips with other artists, Nancy drummed up more illustrating business for her husband. This was the great age of illustration; because photographs could not yet be easily reproduced, publishers of newspapers, magazines, and books needed drawings, and lots of them. And even though the West was settled, people seemed more eager than ever for pictures of the old frontier days. Thanks to Nancy's knack for making contacts, Charlie would soon have as many illustrating jobs as he could handle—creating Western sketches for magazine covers, short stories, memoirs, and novels.

In New York, too, his career took a completely new turn when he created *Smoking Up*, his first sculpture to be cast into bronze. This statue of a cowboy on a rearing horse is only 12 inches high, but it is so full of life that one can almost hear the little rider whooping and hollering! Six casts were made of *Smoking Up*; one of them would be given as a gift to President Theodore Roosevelt.

Smoking Up

This was just the beginning. Charlie would make many more spectacular and popular bronze statuettes. "I like to stick a lot of action in my pictures. . . ," he wrote, and the same can be said for his sculptures. There are bronc riders, Indian warriors, buffalo hunters. There are wolves prowling, mountain sheep locking horns, mother bears searching for food. Charlie sculpted quiet subjects, too, such as the dignified heads of a Piegan man and woman. His sculptures gave him ideas for his paintings. The paintings, in turn, inspired new bronzes. Often he depicted the same subject in both media.

Charlie had fun with sculpture; he had been doing it all his life. His house in Great Falls was full of miniature people and animals made of wax, clay, and plaster, many of them painted and decorated down to the last detail. In homes throughout Montana, there could be found the wax figures that Charlie made every time he sat down to tell a story. He also used his modeling skills to design Christmas window displays for friends' stores—snow scenes complete with log cabins, tepees, and tiny deer. Even at the height of his career, Charlie was never too busy to sculpt little gifts for children. "Friendship art" an old pal of his once called these creations.

Sleeping Thunder

"Glad to get back? Well, I should say I am," Charlie told a reporter when he returned to Great Falls from New York. Back in his beloved home, from about 1905 until almost the end of his life, he would turn out one masterpiece after another. Many of them reached back into the Native American past. In the watercolor *Sun Worship in Montana*, a Blackfoot mother holds her baby up to the sun and prays for a good life for her child. In *The Medicine Man*, a whole Blackfeet tribe is on the move, its spiritual leader riding up front. The backdrop of this oil painting is the Judith Basin as Charlie first saw it in 1880, when it was still wild.

The Medicine Man was part of a selection of Charlie's best paintings and bronzes that were featured in a one-man show in New York City in 1911. "The West That Has Passed" the artist called his exhibit. It wasn't his first show, but it attracted the most notice so far. The exhibit was such a hit that it would be repeated in years to come in many other cities.

CHAPTER FIVE

Sun

Worship in

Montana

The

Medicine

Man

The Cowboy Artist, now 47 years old, was by this time America's best-loved Western artist. His work, from pictures for calendars to illustrations for books to oil paintings for collectors, was in great demand. One of his bear sculptures was chosen for an important art show in Rome, Italy. No longer did the Russells have to worry about money. But instead of becoming conceited, Charlie was grateful: "Any man that can make a living doing what he likes is lucky, and I'm that."

After his success in New York, Charlie was honored by the state of Montana. He was awarded the job of painting a large mural for a wall in the capitol building in Helena. At first he was nervous about taking on the biggest project of his career—a painting that would measure 12 by 25 feet. He had to raise the ceiling of his studio just to fit the canvas inside!

Charlie chose a historic subject for the mural and titled it *Lewis and Clark Meeting Indians at Ross' Hole*. At that spot near Montana's Bitterroot River, in 1805, Flathead Indians shared their food and traded their horses with the weary explorers.

Charlie and Nancy visited Ross's Hole so Charlie could make an accurate sketch of the background. Completed in 1912, the mural is majestic. The background is a sweep of purple mountains capped with snow. Out on the prairie, Lewis and Clark stand off to one side, while the warriors, on horseback, gather front and center. Charlie focused on the proud Flathead riders because he wanted them to be remembered.

In the early 1900s, conditions were difficult for many Native Americans. There were some tribes who did not even have a reservation of their own. Groups of homeless Cree and Chippewa people often camped outside of Great Falls and other Montana towns. Among the Cree was a man named Young Boy, who had been a friend of Charlie's since the roundup days. The injustice being done to Young Boy's people greatly angered Charlie. One freezing winter he started a drive to raise money for the Indians, who had almost no food. "It

Lewis and Clark Meeting Indians at Ross' Hole

doesn't look very good for the people of Montana if they will set still and see a lot of women and children starve to death," he wrote in the local paper. Then he joined his friend Frank Linderman, a writer and outdoorsman, in urging the government to establish the Rocky Boy Reservation as a permanent home for the landless tribes. Because of their efforts on behalf of the Indians, Charlie and Frank were invited to a powwow as special guests of the Cree leader, Little Bear.

Every summer, Charlie and Nancy escaped the streets of Great Falls and headed to a wilderness area that is now part of Montana's Glacier National Park. There, in 1906 on the shores of Lake McDonald, the Russells had built a

cabin that they called Bull Head Lodge. The cabin became a gathering place for family, friends, and fellow artists. During the warm months, Charlie could paint at his easel on the cabin's little porch. At Bull Head Lodge, he was surrounded by nature. The Rocky Mountains gleamed in the distance. The lake sparkled. The cool pine forests were full of animals, large and small. Charlie never went hunting, though, because he couldn't bear to kill any animals. He didn't even mind the skunks who had made a home under his house. They "seem to like the place," he wrote in a humorous letter to a friend. ✳

Although writing was a struggle for Charlie, throughout his life he still sent letters to his wide circle of friends. All wonderfully illustrated—even the envelopes, they were another form of friendship art.

"MEMORIES' TRAILS"

Charlie delighted in stories—in hearing them and telling them as well as in bringing them to life in paint and clay. In 1907 he had begun a new project—writing and illustrating Western yarns for a sports magazine called *Outing*. Putting words on paper was almost as hard for Charlie in 1907 as it had been when he was in school, so he dictated his tales to Nancy, who wrote them down. In 1916 he started another batch of stories, narrated by a Western character that he called Rawhide Rawlins. Later, in the 1920s, the stories would be collected and published in two books, *Rawhide Rawlins Stories* and *More Rawhides*. "Paper talk" is how Charlie thought of his writing, and the public liked it as much as they liked his art.

"I have tried to write some of these yarns as nearly as possible as they were told to me," stated Charlie. In his cowboy slang, he relates things that happened "in the good old days long ago. . . ." A boy runs away from home and is adopted by a Piegan chief. A nightherding cowboy is killed in a stampede. There is a showdown between a mild-mannered sheepherder and a cow town bully, who is as "touchy as a teased snake." And in the story

"Ghost Horse," Charlie tells the legend of his horse Monte's early years, how the animal was stolen from Crow Indians by Piegans before finally being sold to young Charlie.

Although writing was a struggle for Charlie, throughout his life he still sent letters to his wide circle of friends. All wonderfully illustrated—even the envelopes—they were another form of friendship art. Like his pictures and stories, they contain a mix of humor and serious thoughts. He even tried poetry, as in this simple verse he jotted down in a friend's book:

> *The West is dead my friend*
> *But writers hold the seed*
> *And what they sow will live and grow*
> *Again to those who read.*

Charlie's fame took him away from Montana much more often than he liked. Almost until the end of his life, he and Nancy would dash around the country, from one big-city exhibit to another. In 1914 "The West That Has Passed" exhibit traveled to London, England. The Russells went with it, and Charlie gained international acclaim. Many of those who bought the Cowboy Artist's paintings and bronzes were wealthy businessmen, bankers, cattlemen, oil company directors, and politicians. In following years, presidents and royalty, including England's Prince of Wales, would own pictures by Russell. But Charlie's grand new friends did not change him at all. He still wore his red sash and cowboy boots everywhere, even to the fanciest parties, and he still spent time with companions from his Judith Basin days. "Nobody is important enough to feel important," Charlie once said. And he meant it.

He worked constantly. Often he had two or three paintings in progress at the same time. Many of his fans were eager for scenes of fast action and danger. Charlie gave them exciting scenes of men chasing animals and animals chasing men. There were buffalo hunts and wild horse roundups, while in the picture *Crippled But Still Coming*, a wounded grizzly bear is trying to attack a cowboy.

Now in his fifties, Charlie looked more than ever to the past. Through his art he tried to "keep memories' trails fresh." The painting *When the Land Belonged to God* takes the viewer back to the buffalo days. The herd stretches as far as the eye can see, and the Missouri River gleams like gold in the dying light. This painting is one of many in which Charlie uses color and a quiet mood to express his strong love for the land, the sky, the animals—all the wild things.

"This country to day [sic] is fenced and settled by ranch men and farmers with nothing but a few deep worn trails where once walked the buffalo. . . ," Charlie wrote. He sculpted the vanished beasts as well as most of the other animals that he knew from the mountains, forests, and plains of Montana. His bronzes were as sought after as his paintings.

As busy as the Russells were, they found time to welcome two important new people into their lives. In 1916 a young artist named Joe DeYong came to study painting with Charlie. Joe would live in the Great Falls house for months at a time and become almost like a son to Charlie and Nancy. In 1916, too, the Russells adopted a baby boy, whom they named Jack Cooper Russell. It wouldn't be long before Charlie was telling Jack about the cowboys of the Old West and teaching him how to ride a horse.

In 1920 the Russells began spending winters in the warmer climate of southern California. Each year they rented a house either in Pasadena, near Los Angeles, or in Santa Barbara, a bit farther north. Even then, Hollywood was the movie capital of the world. Talkies had not yet been invented, so films were silent. And Westerns were all the rage. Charlie was amused by the way moviemakers stretched the truth about frontier life. Still he loved to visit film *When* sets and watch the action. Movie people asked him for advice because he was *the Land* the real thing: a walking library of facts about the lives and ways of cowboys *Belonged* and Indians on the frontier. *to God*

Smoke of a .45

Charlie made many friends in Hollywood. Some of them were movie stars, such as Tom Mix and Bill Hart, and Will Rogers, who had started out as a trick roper in a Wild West show. Actors Douglas Fairbanks and Mary Pickford met Charlie when they bought one of his paintings. In California, Charlie also met John Ford, one of the world's finest directors of Westerns. Ford looked to Russell and other great Western artists for ideas for his movies. And Charlie's pictures still inspire directors. A good example is his oil painting *Smoke of a .45*. It depicts cowboys shooting up a saloon in a dusty frontier town—a familiar scene even in Westerns today!

Success and honors followed Charlie in the early 1920s. His picture of the fur-trading days, *Salute of the Robe Trade*, sold for $10,000—an almost unheard-of price at the time. In 1925 he received an honorary degree from the University of Montana. Together he and Nancy had crafted an extraordinary life. But as usual, Charlie felt that he was just lucky, rather than anybody special: "To have talent is no credit to its owner; what man can't help he should get neither credit nor blame for—it's not his fault."

There was sorrow in his life, too. By this time many of Charlie's closest friends had died. "Thirty-seven years I've lived in Montana, but I'm among strangers now," he wrote in a letter. His own health was also poor. During an operation on his thyroid in 1926, doctors discovered that his heart was in extremely bad shape. There came the day when Charlie knew he would never ride a horse again. Nancy tried hard to keep her husband's spirits up, and he managed to keep on working for a while. But late on the night of October 24, in their house in Great Falls, Charlie died of a heart attack. He was 62 years old.

"He left us, Nancy, but he *left us much*," wrote Will Rogers. The Cowboy Artist's paintings and drawings number in the thousands. He made countless wax and clay sculptures and 46 models that were cast into bronze. He wrote hundreds of illustrated letters and dozens of stories. And he left behind friends who prized their memories of him even more than his art.

Charles Marion Russell came to Montana in a stagecoach and lived to see the age of the airplane. He arrived in the West in time to see the very last days of the buffalo, the last days of the frontier, and he lived long enough to see those days recreated in the movies. As a boy in St. Louis, he had dreamed a Western dream, and he lived to see it come true. His art and writing capture the excitement, the danger, the beauty, and the sadness of the world he knew. And even though the West changed greatly during Charlie's years there, his love for it never did. "You may lose a sweetheart," he once wrote, "but you won't forget her." ✷

*Charles M.
Russell and
His Friends*

ON THE TRAIL OF THE COWBOY ARTIST

Charles M. Russell National Wildlife Refuge, Montana

In the prairie wilderness of east-central Montana, there is a million-acre wildlife refuge named after Charlie Russell. It protects many species of animals, from prairie dogs to deer, antelope, elk, and bighorn sheep, as well as a wide variety of fish and birds.

Glacier National Park, Montana

Within this vast park, on the shores of Charlie's beloved Lake McDonald, there is a hotel called Lake McDonald Lodge. Its lobby contains a deep fireplace alcove that is decorated with American Indian-style carvings by Russell, who was a frequent visitor.

Great Falls, Montana

Charlie Russell's home and studio in Great Falls now form the C. M. Russell Museum, which has the world's largest collection of Russell's work and memorabilia. The museum also features works by other Western artists and exhibits devoted to Western history.

Helena, Montana

Charlie's great mural, *Lewis and Clark Meeting Indians at Ross' Hole*, can still be seen in the Montana State House of Representatives building.

More Museum Collections of Russell's Art

Amon Carter Museum, Fort Worth, Texas

Buffalo Bill Historical Center, Cody, Wyoming

Colorado Springs Fine Art Center, Colorado Springs, Colorado

The Thomas Gilcrease Institute of American History and Art,
   Tulsa, Oklahoma

Montana Historical Society, Helena, Montana

Museum of Western Art, Denver, Colorado

National Cowboy Hall of Fame and Western Heritage Center,
   Oklahoma City, Oklahoma

Sid Richardson Collection of Western Art, Fort Worth, Texas

Washington, D.C.

In National Statuary Hall, in the nation's Capitol building, there is
a seven-foot-tall statue of Charlie Russell. He is the only artist represented
among the statues of presidents and other famous Americans.

INDEX